Talking Digital

Talking Digital
Conversations with Publishing Executives

DOUGLAS B. HEBBARD

Publisher of TalkingNewMedia.com

TNM Digital Media LLC • Chicago, Illinois

Published by TNM Digital Media LLC

Copyright 2014

The author maintains copyright for his or her respective work

Notice of rights

All rights reserved. This book may not be reproduced in whole or in part, in any form or by any means, electronic or mechanical, including photocopying, recording or by any information storage and retrieval system now known or hereafter invented, without permission from the publisher.

For permission requests, write to the publisher "Attention: Permissions" to the following address:

TNM Digital Media LLC
704 Sun Lake Rd.
Lake Villa, IL 60046

Or visit the TNMDM website at www.TNMDigitalMedia.com

ISBN-13: 9781495213540
ISBN-10: 1495213544

There is one more thing...

— Steve Jobs

CONTENTS

Foreword		i
Chapter One	The iSlate	Pg 7
Section 1	Bonnier & Mag+	Pg 9
Section 2	Sporting News	Pg 19
Section 2	Nomad Editions	Pg 29
Chapter Two	Extensions	Pg 45
Section 1	The Boston Globe	Pg 47
Section 2	The Nation	Pg 53
Section 3	Focus Publishing	Pg 61
Chapter Three	Building A Digital Business	Pg 67
Section 1	TRVL and PRSS	Pg 69
Section 2	Citygram	Pg 79
Section 3	Liz Castro & ePub	Pg 85
Section 4	Joe Zeff Design	Pg 99
Chapter Four	The Rest	Pg 115
Section 1	Known Unknowns	Pg 117
Section 2	About the Author	Pg 122

FOREWORD

Talking Digital consists of interviews with publishing executives from the newspaper, magazine, book publishing and design communities. The source for these interviews, for the most part, was TalkingNewMedia.com – the digital media website I launched in early 2010. A few of the interviews were conducted later as a follow-up to previously written articles.

I sincerely appreciate the cooperation given me when conducting these interviews. Whether conducted in the middle of their efforts, or after a period of time that has allowed for some perspective, each gives advice, encouragement, or a warning to those of us launching our own digital publishing products.

TNM, as I sometimes call the website, was launched when, after nearly 30 years in the newspaper and magazine business, I found myself without a gig. At the time of its conception, late 2009, there were many rumors concerning Apple and its mysterious tablet, the *iSlate*.

Sensing a possible new, important moment in digital publishing I launched Talking New Media as a news and opinion blog in January of 2010, about three weeks before the Apple event introducing the iPad.

I wish I could say that I was omnipotent and knew that the launch of the iPad would be an important moment. But I was driven more by fear. I admit that I initially missed the importance of the iPhone launch. I simply wasn't that interested in Apple's plans for the mobile phone market. But weeks after the launch event I watched Apple's video of the Steve Jobs keynote, it was definitely an "ah ha" moment.

That first iPhone was quite a crippled device, even if it was revolutionary. The original iPhone used Edge for data, making web surfing rather painful. It also only allowed for a limited number of apps. The real revolution took place the day Apple rolled out iOS 2 – and with it third party apps. The era of mobile publishing had begun.

That is why the launch of an Apple tablet *had* to be important.

So to keep up with developments, to be in the middle of things, I launched my blog using Google's Blogger platform.

I suppose the *talking* part of the blog's name came to mind from those early sixties folk songs by Bob Dylan and Phil Ochs that were titled *Talking World III Blues* or *Talking Cuban Crisis*.

I never believed the site would last longer than a few months, but it certainly did and in 2013 the site migrated off of Blogger and onto the WordPress platform.

For those of us in this business – newspapers, magazines and book publishing – looking back is more than just nostalgia. To recognize where we are today and what the future holds, it is important to know the steps that were taken to get here. So this eBook contains interviews with publishing executives *in medias res,* if you will.

Interviews are organized, somewhat artificially, into three sections. **Chapter 1** features three companies at the forefront of tablet publishing following (and in one case before) the launch of the iPad.

The interview with the executives at Mag+ looks back at the origins of the company, but was conducted very early in the company's existence. Everything felt new and the challenge ahead was convincing magazine publishing professionals that investing in the tablet platform was a worthwhile investment. By September of 2012, just under a year after the first interview with a Mag+ executive was conducted, the company already had been responsible for the release of over 600 media apps.

But as much as the Mag+ journey may look like a straight line, the tale of *Sporting News* has been quite different. When I first spoke to Jeff Price he had just recently been named president and publisher of the venerable sports publication. Price had come over from *Sports Illustrated* where he was head of digital. Price had many challenges in front of him, and the zig-zag path the 124-year old publication would take after our interview is pretty amazing to behold.

The interview with Mark Edmiston, the CEO of Nomad Editions, was conducted more recently. Talking New Media had written about the digital magazine start-up many times since its launch in 2010, but none of the posts or interviews seemed to put the whole story together. Most importantly, what had Edmiston learned in the last three years? So a new interview was conducted.

Chapter 2 contains three interviews conducted more recently with established print brands that have begun launching digital-only products as a way of both extending their brands, and utilizing the rich archive of editorial material they possess.

The *Boston Globe* and *The Nation* both have launched new, branded eBook lines that are opening up tremendous opportunities to experiment with both content and form. Focus Publishing, which publishes a quarterly fine art print magazine, began to launch new digital magazines, both for itself and for the artist community it serves.

What ties the three interviews and articles together is the tremendous enthusiasm each media outlet exhibits towards their new digital ventures. In fact, if there is one common theme to this eBook, it might be that the more a media firm embraces digital-only ventures the more enthusiastic and optimistic they are about their chances for success. Nothing can depress one more than talking to a media executive about digital publishing when that executive is embracing digital solely to save their print brands.

Chapter 3 includes four interviews with companies or individuals associated with digital-only ventures (though Liz Castro still produces print books).

The first section of the chapter involves an interview I conducted with the publishing team behind the TRVL iPad magazine app. The digital-only travel magazine has enjoyed wide recognition within the Apple App Store, and later the Newsstand. But now the publishers have made a major change: moving from one digital publishing platform to another – one they have created themselves.

The interview with Chris Perez was included because it exemplifies the often-overlooked trend occurring in the magazine publishing industry: digital-only start-ups that go unnoticed by the traditional print magazine trade press. *Citygram* is a city magazine launched by one individual who believes the digital publication can compete with any legacy print magazine - we shall see.

Finally, this book ends with two digital media authorities who operate in completely different universes, yet have much in common. Liz Castro is an eBook author and publisher who is an authority on EPUB, and is probably that platform's biggest advocate.

Joe Zeff, with his firm Joe Zeff Design, works pretty much exclusively with the Adobe Digital Publishing Suite and is an advocate for stand-alone interactive apps.

What these two creative publishing professionals have in common is an extensive tenure in print publishing, a deep knowledge of their platforms, and endless – though not naive – enthusiasm for the future of digital publishing.

A quick note on the book itself:

This book is the print edition of the original book which was created digitally first (print second). A Kindle Edition is also available, as well as in interactive edition in the Apple iBooks Store.

DOUGLAS B. HEBBARD

Chapter One: The iSlate

Gregg Hano, CEO, Mag+

Section One: Bonnier and Mag+

In the fall and winter of 2009 rumors were rampant about a possible new product from Apple.

"With rumors of the Apple tablet reaching new highs, MacRumors has found evidence that Apple acquired the domain name iSlate.com presumably in preparation for the new device," MacRumors reported on Christmas Eve.

Only a couple weeks later, MacRumors had stumbled upon something else:

"A lot has been said about the rumored Apple tablet, and after evidence was discovered that Apple was interested in the name "iSlate", many have adopted that as the most likely name for Apple's new device…New evidence however has revealed that Apple may, in fact, be positioning "iPad" as the name for the imminent tablet device."

Whatever the product would be called, the publishing industry was pretty sure Apple would be launching a tablet and that this would seriously impact their publishing business.

In the fall of 2009, Apple was meeting with publishers, and word was leaking out:

"Two people related to the NYTimes have separately told me that in June, paper (sic) was approached by Apple to talk about putting the paper on a 'new device.' The R&D labs have long worked on versions of the paper meant to be navigated without a keyboard or mouse, showing up on Windows tablets and on multiple formats using Adobe Air," Gizmodo reported in September of 2009.

With publishers aware that tablets were coming, a few early attempts were made to visualize what their products would look like on a tablet device. One of the most famous of these was created by The Wonderfactory for *Sports Illustrated* magazine.

Another video that appeared around the same time came from the Swedish headquartered magazine company Bonnier and the London design consultancy BERG. That video, which made its way onto YouTube, was the result of work being done by Bonnier Research & Development.

The video featured Jack Schulze of BERG and unveiled the name of Mag+ for the first time to the public. The Mag+ platform, which enables magazine publishers to create interactive digital magazines, originated from work started in 2009, and led to the launch of one of the first interactive digital magazines for Bonnier's *Popular Science* in April of 2010.

One year later Mag+ was spun off to become its own company.

The Mag+ platform is based on a free plug-in that works with InDesign, allowing publication designers and developers to design their tablet editions and apps.

I interviewed Mike Haney, Chief Product Officer at Mag+ in 2011 about the origins of the platform, and in 2012 I interviewed Gregg Hano, who had then just been named CEO of the company. What follows is a melding of those two interviews. Both talk quickly and informally about the history of the Mag+ digital publishing platform.

Gregg Hano:

In mid-2009 an article was in *Popular Science's* "What's New" section on the coming of tablets, and I remember seeing that. I went over to Mark Jannot, who is the editorial director of the Tech group, and I'm like "is this for real?" And he's like "absolutely. No, this is coming, and we think it is coming pretty soon."

I said we needed to get our heads wrapped around what our content is going to look like on tablets.

So we pulled together a small group here – it was myself, Mark Jannot, Sam Syed, the creative director of the Tech group, Mike Haney and Jake Ward – and Haney obviously was with Tech and Jake still is – and we began to conceive what, and how, we would build a digital magazine.

Mike Haney:

At PopSci – because both our publisher Gregg Hano and our editor Mark Jannot are both very forward-looking people, very entrepreneurial, and our creative director, Sam Syed, is that way as well – so we had already, even in the couple years before tablets really came on, started to look at what digital publishing might mean.

At that time, our context was Zinio, which was our

platform — PDF replicas which we'd been doing for years like every other publisher, sort of switching between Texterity and Zinio and the desktop, because tablets really weren't there yet in any real way. We had started looking at the iPhone but really had trouble wrapping our brains around how a magazine, especially like PopSci – infographic heavy, information dense – would translate to the iPhone. So really our frame of reference was the desktop.

Sam really started exploring what more could you do with Zinio as a platform – they were starting to add some interactivity, some Flash-based things to it – and what happens if you start designing, if you use this platform and design things specifically for the screen they are going to be consumed on.

Gregg Hano:

We at that time partnered with Zinio to develop three — our original goal was four – three magazines for screens. It was, of course, for laptops at the time.

Two of them were not particularly good, I must admit.

But the third one was called Greening Your Home Guide (The Green Home Guide), how to make your home environmentally friendly – and we put video in there, and links, and some service, and we got a sponsor, Eveready batteries sponsored it. We were really happy with that product.

So at a Bonnier conference, some time later, we shared that product, and as a result of sharing it with other international publishers we were connected with the Bonnier

R&D team in Stockholm who had also been thinking about what to do in the space.

The woman who directs R&D here is Sara Öhrvall. Sarah and the R&D team had been thinking about this.

What they then went on to do was develop an international competition between four different Bonnier groups – one magazine from Sweden, one from Denmark, ourselves here in New York, and then our TransWorld team out in Oceanside.

We ended up winning that competition, which ended up being the beta for Mag+.

Mike Haney:

There were about five or six magazines, across the company globally, where there was an editor and a designer who were part of this early concept and research phase."

The fall of that year (2009) was when we kicked off the project – Sara Öhrvall, head of R&D moved from Stockholm to San Francisco – we started doing conceptual work. At the same time, we contracted with a firm in London, digital design firm, BERG – a brilliant, brilliant, little firm – and sort of tasked them with doing the same thing along side us.

So we're coming at it as magazine makers and thinking in our space, and they're coming at it as digital designers because they really know the digital space. And all of us are wrestling with what should the magazine be and doing these conceptual exercises.

How do you represent a story? What does it mean when

Mike Haney, Chief Creative Officer, Mag+

you can touch? What does it mean when your page is much smaller?

So that video is really the product of that work. That was the product of that first three or four months.

Really our idea behind that was 'we're doing all this stuff, let's put it (the video) out on the Internet and see what people think. What we got from that was a lot of validation that the ways we were thinking about this were resonating with people.

They understood the idea that a magazine experience shouldn't just be a PDF.

I worked on this project, in its early phases, still as executive editor of *Popular Science*.

When the iPad was announced (late January of 2010), we decided that day – 'we know what we want to do, we've done the video, the concept work is done, all we've got to do now is build it' – we decided that day, let's build it, let's try to be there at launch, and let's launch with PopSci because both Sam and I were the ones who were most involved.

We were really tight with it; it seemed like the perfect title within the Bonnier stable to intersect with those early adopters.

By the time we launched I was spending half my time with this project and not doing my full time job as executive editor, so I left PopSci at that time and went to the R&D department and spent most of last year, from April to the end of the year, in the R&D department – mostly focusing on

Mag+ but doing some other projects, as well.

Then when Mag+ was spun off into an independent company this year, I left both PopSci and the R&D department and joined the new company.

Update:

Mag+ was spun off from Bonnier on April 4, 2011.

Staffan Ekholm, the company's original CEO wrote of the new company: "Mag+ was created by publishers for publishers. We boast a superb leadership and development team, with a breadth of experience in both digital and publishing. The team has already taken more than 25 magazine titles on to iPads, with others lining up in markets including the US, the UK, and across the Continent."

One year later, on April 12, 2012, Gregg Hano was named the new CEO of Mag+.

By September of 2013 Hano was able to say that the Mag+ platform has been used on more than 1,500 apps for more than 700 clients in more than 80 countries.

TALKING DIGITAL

Sporting News on the iPad

Section Two: Sporting News

In February 2010, American City Business Journals, a division of Advance Publications, announced that it had hired Jeff Price to be the new publisher of *Sporting News*, its venerable sports publication.

Price had left Time Inc. in April of the previous year where he was president of SI Digital, the digital arm of *Sports Illustrated*.

"I kind of feel like I got the first pick in the NFL draft or just landed the best free agent on the market," Whitney Shaw, ACBJ chief executive, said in the hiring announcement.

"Either way, this is big for Sporting News. There's not a more qualified person than Jeff Price to help us continue to build *Sporting News*. He's bright, he's connected and he's totally dedicated to what we're doing."

Bringing on someone from the digital side of a competitor to be the new publisher clearly meant the publication would be transforming itself for the digital media era.

But, in many ways, that transformation was well on its way before Price arrived.

Shortly after being acquired by American City Business Journals, *The Sporting News* launched an emailed daily publication called Sporting News Today. Staci D. Kramer, then at paidContent.org, called it a "digital Hail Mary play" as the publication was seen as badly trailing its big competitors, *Sports Illustrated* and *ESPN The Magazine*.

The new owner also cut the frequency of the main product from weekly to bi-monthly. (And somewhere in all this it officially changed the name of the magazine from *The Sporting News* to just *Sporting News*.)

At the time I interviewed Price early in May of 2010, Sporting News Today was a free online digital flipbook that Price wanted to transform into a paid product. Additionally, Price would have to consider what the impact of the recently released iPad might be on his business.

At first, the strategy was about creating products that could be read on multiple devices. "We really like the idea that we could charge the consumer $2.99 per month no matter what device they engaged with it on," Price said at the time.

New Sporting News publisher, Jeff Price, partners with Zinio on paid daily iPad and web-based news products

It hasn't taken the new President and Publisher of *Sporting News* long to make a big impact on the venerable brand: developing partnerships, transforming free products to paid, and launching apps. For Jeff Price, the former head of digital for *Sports Illustrated*, it is all about building the brand and extending the reach of the publication.

Price comes to the 124-year-old *Sporting News* with a marketing and sports background, and sees his role more as brand champion than publisher. But for a publication that was last dominate when John McGraw still managed the Giants (OK, slight exaggeration) the challenges of transforming the title into a major player in both electronic and print media will be great.

With the help of one of his new media partners, Zinio, I talked to Price about his New Media plans and the ground already covered since the announcement of his appointment in February by the owner of *Sporting News*, American City Business Journal, a unit of Advance Publications Inc.

Price has moved immediately by making some hard decisions at *Sporting News*. These included ending the title's fantasy games operation, the source of some of the title's best web traffic.

"The fantasy industry is changing, and we feel it's best to devote our resources to providing the best fantasy content and advice on the Internet, and beyond," Price wrote in a letter to customers.

Price had made the same move at *Sports Illustrated*, where he was head of digital, before relaunching the service. Price said he would be doing the same thing at *Sporting News*, launching a new fantasy games service in time for football season, this time with an unannounced, major new media partner.

Creating partnerships is part of Price's M.O., as business development was part of the job description for Price at previous stops at Millsport, Trakus, MasterCard and USA Sports.

One of the most important new partnerships Price

established was with Zinio, the San Francisco headquartered digital magazine and book company. Price decided to work with his new partner on Sporting News Today, the publication's daily web-based newspaper, rather than the main biweekly *Sporting News* magazine.

"Part of the struggle that's going on right now in the industry is trying to force fit what your current business model is into this new platform," Price said.

"If we were taking that approach we would have started with *Sporting News* magazine and said 'OK, we're going to put all our energy behind *Sporting News* magazine and we're going to translate that over to the iPad.'"

Rather than have Zinio port over their bi-weekly magazine, Price would have his new partner bring the previously free Sporting News Today daily to the iPad (as well as other mobile formats), through Zinio's digital newsstand. Now, a reader can subscribe to the daily product and read their news on an iPad, or on the web, and just pay once – currently 99 cents an issue, or $2.99 a month.

For now, readers of *Sporting News*, the magazine, will have to wait for an iPad solution.

"We've honestly put that on the shelf for now and we'll come back to that and find a way to make sure that its available for those folks who'd want to engage with the magazine from a digital content perspective."

One advantage of starting with Sporting News Today was that it was already a digital-only product. The other reason was that Price saw that the product filled an important need for consumers. Sporting News Today "was providing packaged content on a daily basis, 365 days a year, really giving a comprehensive review of what happened yesterday in sports and being ready for consumers and business travelers at 6 am in the morning --- we really looked at the opportunity that we had was to fill a void that folks in the newspaper sector are certainly trying to do," Price said.

Working with Zinio provided *Sporting News* the opportunity to have first mover advantage. Price had seen that, on the iPhone and Android, app developers had leaped into the field -- apps like Sportacular and SportsTap were "thinking like start-ups" by providing readers the sports information they wanted on their mobile devices -- they took advantage of the opening created when publishers failed to step up and rethink their products.

Price's appointment as president and publisher at *Sporting News* occurred shortly after Steve Jobs introduced the iPad at a media event in San Francisco. Price was paying attention to the video demonstrations other media firms were producing for hypothetical tablet products.

"The first buzz came out around the S.I. demo and what was done -- and I used to work at S.I. for a long time so I was very familiar with what they were doing -- we just thought this editorial engine that we had (in the daily Sporting News Today product) had a better chance to solve the consumer need in the space," Price said.

"So we spent a long time talking to a number of potential partners on the back end, because we recognized that 'hey, we're not a technology company' . . . We didn't want to just have an iPad strategy, we wanted to have an overall strategy -- that no matter where the consumer wanted to engage in content we were going to create the opportunity to be there for them. And Zinio was really the only potential back-end partner. They came with a comprehensive strategy that was certainly inclusive of iPad as a major game-changer in the space, but was not just solely focused on delivering the iPad."

"The other piece that was interesting to us, since we moved from a free product to a subscription product, was the idea that we'd be able to charge the consumer $2.99 a month no matter what device they engaged with it on," Price said.

Sporting News Today will come out with its own branded app some time this summer, again working with Zinio. The app will be able to take advantage of another one of the recently negotiated partnerships -- this one with CineSport, a company that offers web video syndication of sports highlights and on-demand video.

"We will be bringing our highlight content, both national and local market content, into the iPad experience -- as well as across every device where we deliver Sporting News Today," Price promises. "So that partnership (with CineSport) becomes a critical component of what we do to improve the overall experience. If you are a commuter walking onto a train -- you're a displaced fan, a business traveler, a college student, the key folks we're going after -- we feel we can create a multimedia sports experience. You're no longer tethered to your TV set waiting for Sports Center . . . that is really a huge point of difference in the sports category for what we see being planned from the magazine set, so to speak."

I asked Zinio about the idea of working with publishers on dedicated apps as this seemed like a new area for the company. "We are exploring design enhancements and the potential of publisher-specific, co-branded entry points to the Zinio app," confirmed Jeanniey Mullen, Global EVP and CMO, at Zinio.

Zinio's iPad app appeared in the iTunes app store the day of the iPad launch. Both Zinio, and those publishers working with the company, have benefited by the decision to be there on Day One. "The reader response is phenomenal," Mullen said, "as evidenced by the Zinio App for iPad, which has remained in the top-10 in the news category, after it spiked to #1 within the first week of launch."

All these changes will have to be monetized, of course, but Price is looking long term, preferring to have his team work with the advertising community to experiment with these new products, and learn from the experience and customer feedback. The Sporting News Today web and iPad product currently has advertising from Coors Light embedded.

One of the more fundamental changes made so far has been to reorganize the sales team. There is now a national head of print sales, Paul Severini, who will be responsible for *Sporting News* and Sporting News Today. They also named a digital advertising director, Joey Glowacki, who will head sales for the web, mobile, interactive television, and fantasy games.

One thing the team has learned is that print ad people are very interested in tablet products because the user experience is much more like print.

"The creative canvas is much more in-line with the canvas that print creatives have been working with, than digital creatives," Price observes.

"We're not talking about 300 by 250 units, we're not talking about skyscrapers, we're talking about pages and spreads. Now add to that the ability to bring in rich media and video and interactivity, and you have some of the same tools that have existed in the digital space but there in an environment that is much more like print than anything we've seen today."

For Price, the introduction of new mobile products is an opportunity for a publication to rethink their products and to reorient them towards their customer's needs. To this end, Price said the SportingNews.com website will be redesigned and re-imagined as much more of a breaking news vehicle. Eventually, the daily product, SNT, may stand on its own once it has reached a critical mass.

"I think we're missing the boat if we don't completely re-imagine what the opportunity is with our brands. This is my own problem with many of the folks within the publishing industry. They talk about titles instead of thinking about brands. We've really tried to think about our brand," Price said.

"We're trying to think like a 124-year-old start-up," Price said. "There were two or three players (referring back to Sportacular and SportsTap) who stepped into the sports space and became players in mobile out of nowhere, simply because they thought about the consumer and not about the way you force your own business into the model and your own kind of legacy issues."

Price promises to keep things fresh as they roll out their new products and partnerships this summer, and well into the fall football season.

(Originally published on TalkingNewMedia.com on May 7, 2010)

Mark M. Edmiston – courtesy of Nomad Editions

Section Three: Nomad Editions

One of the most interesting publishing company launches of the last few years has been Nomad Editions, a digital magazine start-up founded by publishing veteran Mark M. Edmiston.

Nomad Editions seemed to have everything going for it: a magazine veteran at its head, one with plenty of business acumen; $600,000 in initial funding; a recognized design guru helping with the concept; and plenty of media coverage to drive awareness.

Things have not turned out quite as its founders would have predicted. But the story is far from over for Nomad Editions.

Mark M. Edmiston started at Time Inc. working on consumer marketing for *LIFE* magazine and then *The Saturday Review*, before becoming the publisher of Psychology Today. Edmiston joined *Newsweek* as circulation director of the international editions in 1973 and eventually worked his way up to President/CEO of *Newsweek* in 1981.

In 1992 he co-founded The Jordan, Edmiston Group, a leading mergers and acquisitions company in the media space. He left that company and joined AdMediaPartners in 1999 where he was involved in quite a number of major media deals before his retirement from the company in 2009.

That leads us to Nomad Editions. Nomad was started in 2009 with partner Marjorie W. Martay as a way to launch digital magazines for reading on multiple devices. From 2009 to 2012, the direction of the company evolved quickly – from one inspired by the iPhone, to one driven by HTML5, to one dedicated to iPad publishing. In just over three years Nomad Editions has ridden the digital publishing roller coaster like few companies have.

What follows is an attempt to tell the story based on the two interviews I conducted with Edmiston – in early 2012 and then again in July of 2013. Inserted into parts of the story as told by Edmiston are excerpts of articles and press releases from the time of the launch to the company today.

The Idea

The germ of an idea for what became Nomad Editions started when Mark Edmiston was asked by Marjorie Martay to take a meeting.

"We really started in September-October of 2009. My partner, who is still my partner, knew a guy at Condé Nast who had been pretty much laid off from being full-time to a contributing editor," Edmiston said. "He was looking for ways to make some money, had an idea, and wasn't sure what to do with it. And so my partner, Marjorie, asked me if I would talk to him, and so we did. We both talked to him."

"It was a very interesting idea. Obama had just been elected, and he was a political journalist and so he was going to write about Obama, follow Obama – and it would be called the Obama Blog or something."

But rather than simply create a blog, the editor said he had a twist.

"But he was going to charge for it, he was going to turn it into an app and charge for it, as opposed to just doing a blog," said Edmiston. "I think he was going to charge $7.99 a month or something like that and he would update this on a regular basis."

"So we talked to him and at first tried to expand his idea because it occurred to me that this was a perfectly OK idea for one individual but really was not a business. Because, for the next subject matter, you would have to start from scratch again. So you're starting a bunch of little companies instead of something that could scale up to a big company."

Eventually the idea came to nothing, but it did spur Martay and Edmiston to think about launching a company. At first, because he was an iPhone user, the emphasis was on mobile reading.

"The iPhone is what attracted me. I starting reading books, then the only things really available, on my iPhone. It wasn't the greatest, but it really wasn't all that bad, either. You could read on these things."

But then Roger Black came into the picture.

Black is a well-known newspaper and magazine publications designer, who was once described by Michael Wolff as having "many character traits in common with the Claude Rains character Louis Renault, the police captain in Casablanca."

Black is famous for his work with *The Los Angeles Times*, *Rolling Stone*, *Esquire*... and *Newsweek*.

"We officially formed the company in 2010 and worked with Roger Black who had an idea that I hadn't even thought about. I was thinking of doing apps. He was saying 'you really need HTML5, and I got this brilliant guy who used to be a Microsoft engineer and he can do it.'"

The result was the original publishing platform that was unique to Nomad Editions called Treesaver. A web-based system, the platform would create online magazines that could be read on any device: desktop, smartphone or tablet. It was, in other words, responsive design.

The Concept

Along side the design platform was a unique way to pay editors. Editors would be paid based on the number of subscribers they could attract. At first the plan, as described in the first article to appear about the company, was a bit complicated: writers would receive a cut of revenue while editors received a smaller cut, but also a cut of the advertising.

The plan as implemented was simpler.

"The compensation scheme was a revenue share, 35 percent to the editor," Edmiston said. "But we did provide a stipend to start off. We paid the editors $2,000 a month and we gave the editor $1,000 an issue to distribute to his contributors as he wished. It was his responsibility – his or her's – to go out and find the people, the right stories, and basically assemble the magazine."

What was also different was the publishing cycle. Rather than publishing monthly, Nomad Editions magazines would be weekly – and smaller in size.

"We were so early in the process that we had to invent things," Edmiston said. "One thing that we invented was the fact that it (the magazines) was not going to be a reproduction of another magazine, it was not going to be a digital replica. We would write original material designed from the beginning to be on a mobile device."

"That meant it should be shorter. No scientific research here at all, but we said 'well, a monthly magazine has about 100 editorial pages, let's put the equivalent of 25 editorial pages in each of our weekly editions.' Which we did."

As explained in a VentureBeat article that appeared when the company launched, Edmiston visualized the new digital magazines as distinctly different from traditional print magazines.

"When TV first came out, one of the things people tried to do was put radio shows on television," Edmiston told VentureBeat.

"Well that didn't work. TV evolved into a different type of medium — and that's what we're doing. Magazines aren't dead. They're evolving. They will look a little different and have a different business model. But we will still be reading them 15 years from now."

Backed by $600,000 in funding from friends, family and angel investors, Nomad Editions was officially launched… at least in theory, as no actual digital magazines were yet available.

Nomad Editions' page design on the iPhone

Next the company began to sign up readers on their website, telling them that they would be notified by email when Nomad would go live. Meanwhile, the Nomad team would begin considering magazine ideas.

"We would sit down at a round table and journalists would propose these ideas and we would talk about them. And then we'd come back to these people who proposed them and say here's the deal. It's a revenue share, we'll give you a little money upfront, but it is a revenue share, and you are responsible for putting your weekly magazine together," Edmiston said.

Readers received their email notice that the magazines were live in December of 2010 with the launch of the first two titles: *Real Eats* and *Wave Lines*.

What had changed since that first meeting in 2009 and the end of 2010 was the launch of the iPad. While the first digital magazines could be read online, and looked awfully good on the iPhone, they were not really designed for the iPad. In fact, if there was a problem with the system, it was that it wasn't designed specifically for any device, but could work on all devices.

"We actually launched in HTML and it was not as successful as I would have liked because it was pretty clunky and the engineer got hired as the CTO at Flipboard, so my key guy was gone!" Things were moving fast in digital publishing. While a print magazine start-up would usually have several years to test out its market, the digital publishing market was evolving fast. In April 2010, Apple shipped its first iPads to US buyers, and six weeks later Apple began taking pre-orders from European buyers.

Real Eats, **one of the first digital magazine titles launched**

Bonnier's *Popular Science* launched its digital edition, using its own Mag+ platform, immediately – and many other major magazine publishers began to follow suit.

To serve iPad owners, Nomad Editions launched its first branded app in May 2011. That app gave readers access to the five titles the company was now producing: *BodySmart, Real Eats, U+Me, Uncorked* and *Wide Screen*, *Wave Lines* having already been dropped.

By November of 2011, after Apple had introduced its Newsstand, the company launched four individual apps for its magazine titles *Uncorked, Real Eats, BodySmart* and *Wide Screen*.

The next move towards more native iPad editions occurred in March of 2012 when the company launched three app updates that moved the digital magazines over to the Mag+ platform.

"The big issue we are facing, which is the problem with everyone going into it, is discovery," Edmiston told me at the time. "There is so much competition out there, it is really important that we try to get the best product. That's why we led ourselves to work with Mag+."

"But our focus is on iOS for the obvious reason, that's where the money is. We feel that Mag+ brings us up to the state-of-the-art in terms of the product itself."

"It's sort of like George Patton – the battle plan is good until you start meeting the enemy – we've changed a lot. Originally when I started thinking about this, back in 2009, before we even formed the company, we were very much focused on the phones. We thought the iPhone was really where we wanted to be."

The Retreat

Discoverability proved to be a problem that Nomad Editions could not overcome, even with the launch of the Newsstand. The magazines needed, Edmiston estimated, around 10,000 subscribers to be viable.

"They didn't come close. They were in the low thousands," Edmiston told me in 2013.

Reaching readers, which at first appears to be eased through the creation of digital newsstands, actually can be more difficult than with print if the right marketing is not employed.

"Basically what we found, this really started in the beginning of 2012, a year and a half ago, it was becoming very, very clear that the only way you could succeed was if Apple promoted you."

"We had one edition that they mentioned us for a day and we got 17,000 orders. These were free trials. Without their mentioning it we were getting hundreds."

"I'd say that right now the App Store, and its subdivision the Newsstand, is a very poor marketplace. And I think that no matter who you are, even if you're willing to spend a huge amount of money – and I think Murdoch proved that. I think supposedly he spent a hundred million dollars in trying to launch *The Daily*, and fell very far short what his number was for circulation – it's not there," Edmiston said.

"The infrastructure is not there to have a good marketplace. It's like going to a huge newsstand some place and you don't know what you're looking for and you start wandering around, and you get stuck in the *Ladies Home Journal* section, or something like that and you can't find your way out."

"What is interesting in retrospect is that if you were to launch a print publication there is a huge infrastructure that already exists out there to find your customers. There are agents, there is direct mail, there are ways of targeting your message to interested parties. You don't have to buy television time."

"With Apple, they will not let you have any direct contact with their customers. There is no way you can promote yourself to this new space, they won't let you do it. You can't buy an ad on the iTunes store. Since that is where the people who are buying digital magazines live for the most part, the overwhelming majority of the market – without being able to buy an ad – there is no way to reach them in any kind of efficient way," Edmiston said.

Nomad Editions was already changing its model a bit in the face of disappointing subscription numbers. The company needed to build digital magazines that could reach an existing, knowable readership.

"So early last year, 2012, we started switching," Edmiston said.

"We said let's rethink this. Maybe what we need to do is instead of creating our own publications and going out and hoping to find people, which is not working, let's think about where people already exist, have identified themselves already, and see if we can work with them and create partnerships. And that was the evolution of the idea. The publications, we'll still produce them on the same basis, with a revenue share."

That led to finding two publishing partners: *Hemmings Motor News* and the Snooth wine website.

"With Snooth, which is still around, we created a monthly publication out of their already existing materials that they had on their website, but reformulated into a magazine-like product. Makes it easier to access. We would focus each month on a grape – you know, Chardonnay, or Grenache, or whatever it is."

"They already had a million registered users. So there are a million people who said 'at least I'll give you my email address' that you can identify them and reach them with an email message – I think something like 750,000 of the million said they would receive email."

The problem, Edmiston found, was that working with established print publishers can be… well, difficult.

"It is probably true that going to publishers, which was one of our ideas, to work with them and create things for publishers, was not a good idea," Edmiston conceded. Though "the Snooth one worked," Edmiston said, "and they are happy with it. "

And so the company made a major announcement in September of 2012: Nomad Editions would shutter its existing three consumer titles.

"After struggling for close to three years, we've decided to discontinue the consumer-facing magazines," Edmiston told *Adweek*.

"The internal numbers are great. We're just not able to get enough subscribers. It's steadily improving. But we're still 20 percent of where we need to be profitable. We need to get to about 10,000 subscriptions."

With their original consumer magazines now folded, one might think that Nomad Editions would simply fold up its tent and move on. But the company now has set a new direction and Edmiston says it is now making money, rather than burning through its investment money.

In November of 2012, Nomad Editions announced in a press release that it would concentrate on content marketing initiatives beginning with a deal with "a major pharmaceutical house".

"Content marketing is not just advertising in a magazine format," said Marjorie Martay, Executive Vice President. "It is engaging readers with compelling editorial in support of the sponsoring company's marketing objectives. Having learned how to acquire and engage targeted consumer bases, we can now apply that knowledge to driving profitable customer action for our clients."

"What we have learned," Edmiston told me, "is that we have to go some place where there is a bunch of customers already. You can't find them through the current digital world. You have to go some place where they have already identified themselves."

"We're approaching different organizations, not just custom publishing kinds of things, where we might launch a partnership and create some publications for them. The one thing we have done over the past three and half years is we've really learned how to do it. And we have people who have a skill set and we believe we can produce these things as efficiently as anybody can at this point, including the big guys."

"We're talking to organizations that have existing databases of customers, and are in the process of negotiating with three of them and hopefully one of the three will come through. We would be back in the consumer publishing market – but with a partner and with a brand that people will recognize."

As for Roger Black, he has left the country, moving to Hong Kong, where he says "print is still robust," to work with Edipresse Asia. There he hopes they get "a chance to get the digital transformation right."

(A much shorter version of this article appeared on TalkingNewMedia.com on July 26, 2013)

Chapter Two: Extensions

The iBooks edition cover for *68 Blocks*

Section One: The Boston Globe

Newspapers produce a wealth of content each week in print, as well as online. But in my own time in the newspaper industry, I found that few metro dailies would leave their comfort zone of producing exclusively the daily paper (and later its website) to begin creating other publishing products.

It was not always like this as many years ago the local newspaper was often also the local printer of brochures and other products for its community. But over the years many newspapers became single product entities, allowing new competitors to appear in their markets.

With the rise of the new digital platforms of mobile and tablets, the opportunity to create brand extensions such as eBook lines and digital magazines means a newspaper, at a low cost, can create new products that can take advantage of the paper's extensive catalog of content.

Tribune Interactive, for instance, produced a series of sports magazines for the *Chicago Tribune*, though that effort was curtailed shortly after it began.

This chapter looks at three publications that have come to recognize that they are sitting on a wealth of great material waiting to be made available again. Two of the publications, the *Boston Globe* and *The Nation*, have launched their own eBook imprints, while the third, Focus Publishing, has launched a digital magazine initiative.

68 Blocks and Boston Globe eBooks

The *Boston Globe* recently released its thirteenth eBook, *68 Blocks*, which originated from a five-day series the newspaper ran about the Dorchester neighborhood of Bowdoin-Geneva.

So few newspapers have become, what I like to call, serial launchers – real publishers rather than merely newspaper companies. Digital media offers that opportunity through not only producing eBooks, but also through mobile media, tablet editions, etc. The *Boston Globe*, which sadly has been put up for sale by The New York Times Co., may become an exception, as the publisher has been very active in experimenting in the eBook publishing area.

Recently I spoke with the newspaper's design director, Dan Zedek, about their eBook efforts

"I would love to say it was months of planning and focus grouping," Zedek said. "But, in fact, when iBooks Author came out... me and one other guy, Javier Zarracina, the graphics director, were really interested in the program. So we said 'this is pretty cool let's try this out.' We both went home over the weekend, downloaded it, and built an eBook."

That eBook, on the Isabella Stewart Gardner Museum, never saw its way into the iBook Store, but Zedek said "we were impressed by the possibilities."

"On Monday morning we pitched it to the editor-in-chief at the time, Marty Baron. 'We'd like to try doing some eBooks' and we just kind of dove in."

In addition to working with Apple's iBooks Author, a free

download inside the Mac App Store, the *Globe* has also been working with freeware and other solutions. These include Calibre, Sigil and Vook.

One of the 13 books released, *Whitey Bulger: America's Most Wanted Gangster and the Manhunt that Brought Him to Justice*, came through working with an outside vendor.

From the get-go, the mission has been to make any eBooks produced available on as many devices as possible, in addition to making them available free of charge to Globe subscribers.

Because of this, the design team has used iBooks Author to produce interactive books for iBooks, as well as to export a PDF for downloading. The editors then produce products for other platforms, such as can be seen with the newest eBook, *68 Blocks: Life, Death, Hope in Boston's Most Troubled Neighborhood*.

The *Globe's* series, which was called 68 Blocks: Life, Death, Hope when first published, was the result of the efforts of a five-person team of reporters who immersed themselves in the Bowdoin-Geneva area in the summer of 2012. The stories generated ran in a five-part series that appeared in December on the *Globe's* website, as well as in the paper.

"We had this really elaborate five-day print project, that was the print iteration of it. We also had a very rich multimedia digital presence for it," Zedek said. "So we were starting with tremendous source material, and we were looking at what we wanted to incorporate (into the eBook), keeping in mind… that there are a lot of different devices, and we want to be a good experience on all those devices."

"So we kind of went in two tracks: we used iBooks Author as a way of displaying the multimedia – we could have done even more actually, but I think it was a pretty rich presentation as it was; at the same time we used Vook to create eBooks that would work on the NOOK, that would work on a Kindle; and we also used iBooks Author to produce a PDF."

Zedek said that two-thirds of the downloads so far have been from iOS eBooks or the PDFs created using iBooks Author, "so it is capturing most of the market for us."

The planned publishing schedule is to produce one new eBook a month on subjects like the Boston band Aerosmith, or on the photography of David Ryan, who has taken shots of the city using a helicopter.

"But at the same time," Zedek says "I'm really interested in pursuing a slightly different approach which is to create pop-out instant books on topics of immediate interest. Because I think with the metabolism that a newspaper has, we're used to working that way, and we can provide a lot of original content very, very quickly.

"I imagine we could do a pretty great book with a really quick turnaround on the day people are thinking about this and looking for more depth and context of the news. How great would it be to have an eBook available for them?"

Zedek used as an example, the upcoming conclave to elect a new pope. The *Globe* has written quite often on the subject and would be able to produce an eBook immediately upon the new pope being identified.

"This whole thing was started as a lab for us, a place for us to experiment with content types, with production types, with different reader groups, and we want to keep pushing that," Zedek said.

"What really excites me about it is continuing to see what we can do to bring value and interest to our readers."

(Originally published on TalkingNewMedia.com on March 6, 2013)

Update:

Since this article appeared, the *Boston Globe* has published two additional eBooks: *The Best of Beverly Beckham* and *Boston By Air* by David L. Ryan.

As for the *Boston Globe* itself, it was announced on August 3, 2013 that The New York Times Company had sold the newspaper to John Henry, the owner of the Boston Red Sox.

The paper was sold for $70 million. The NYT Co. had purchased the paper in 1993 for $1.1 billion.

Section Two: The Nation

The Nation weekly magazine has been publishing continuously since July 1865.

During its history, a great number of amazing writers have contributed to its print magazine pages.

Up until recently, *The Nation's* book publishing activities have been limited to producing print books for journalists who are contributors to the magazine. Many of these eventually were made into Kindle Editions.

Starting in 2013, *The Nation* launched its own line of eBooks with the publication of Gore Vidal's State of the Union, and with it a new subsection of its website that it calls eBookNation.

I was invited in July to preview *Molly Ivins: Letters to The Nation*, the second eBook released under the eBookNation banner.

As part of that effort I spoke to Art Stupar, VP of Circulation at The Nation who leads the new eBook initiative.

The Nation releases its second eBookNation selection: *Molly Ivins: Letters to The Nation*

I must admit that I really miss Molly Ivins, the Texas journalist known for her sharp, biting pen, and her strong stances against political corruption, the war in Iraq, and the domination of Texas by the Republicans. Ivins was a name caller, a provocateur, and all together funny and spot on.

Wikipedia, for instance, wisely includes this quote from Ivins about Bill Clinton:

"If left to my own devices, I'd spend all my time pointing out that he's weaker than bus-station chili. But the man is so constantly subjected to such hideous and unfair abuse that I wind up standing up for him on the general principle that some fairness should be applied. Besides, no one but a fool or a REPUBlican ever took him for a liberal."

Sadly, breast cancer took Molly Ivins away from us too young, at only 62.

Ivins was born in Monterey, California, but that was an accident of birth. Ivins was a Texan through and through – except for that REPUBlican part. She attended Smith and Columbia, and began her career at the *Minneapolis Tribune*, and eventually made her way back to Texas to write for the Texas Observer and then McClatchy's *Fort Worth Star-Telegraph*.

In between, she worked at *The New York Times* where her style and abrasiveness was sorely needed, but not really appreciated.

It was the opportunity to write her own columns that drew her away from the Grey Lady and back to Texas where for ten years she wrote for the *Dallas Times-Herald*.

With the freedom to write columns rather than news stories, Ivins could freelance and let it all hang out. Not surprisingly, her words started to appear in the pages of *The*

Nation. Starting in 1982 with a letter to the editor, Ivins started writing in the political weekly.

Along the way, Ivins tore into the Bushs, the Texas legislature, and just about anything she felt was phony, undemocratic and corrupt.

Now Molly Ivins' words for *The Nation* can live on thanks to the recently launched eBookNation series. *Molly Ivins: Letters to The Nation* is the second eBook released by the political weekly, and it certainly won't be the last.

Priced at $9.99, the eBook is available directly from the publisher on its website where they maintain a new bookstore. (The first of their eBook releases *Gore Vidal's State of the Union*, also priced at $9.99.)

"What we have," Art Stupar VP, Circulation at *The Nation*, told me last week, "is this unbelievable stable of historic writers that have written for us. It's hard to miss when you have people like H.L. Mencken, or Martin Luther King Jr. or James Baldwin writing for you."

To take advantage of this content, the publisher has created an eBook series that wisely attempts to reach as large an audience as possible by making sure readers can access the material no matter what digital reading device they own, or in whatever environment they wish to read.

Both new eBooks can be bought in PDF or EPUB form from *The Nation's* website, but they are also loading into Apple's iBook Store, Amazon.com, Barnes & Noble's NOOK store, and through Kobo.

"I would say this is an outgrowth of our success with digital editions of the magazine," Stupar said.

Nothing like a REPUBlican convention to drive you screaming back into the arms of the Democrats. Especially this convention. The elders of the press corps kept muttering they hadn't seen anything like it since the Goldwater convention in '64. True, the REPUBlicans spent much of their time peddling fear and loathing, but it was more silly than scary, like watching people dressed in bad Halloween werewolf costumes. During the buildup to the convention, the most cockeyed optimists among the Democrats were in hopes the REPUBlicans would tear themselves apart over abortion. No need. The party was dead meat on arrival.
– Notes from Another Country (1992)

"We started back… about three or four years ago. We started first with the Kindle. Then the Barnes & Noble NOOK. Then Sony and the various devices – Apple and so forth."

"We have our own direct to publisher digital edition and that's pretty popular. Then when we reached out to all the other devices we hit it pretty big with the Kindle – NOOK, as well – now with Apple on the iPad, iPhone, and other devices through Zinio. The success of selling our content digitally was really step one."

Step two was creating an online bookstore and stocking it with wonderful material, which for a magazine that was launched in the summer of 1865 shouldn't be too hard.

Like the *Boston Globe*, which has also launched its own eBook series, *The Nation* will be able to access its own archives for material for new publications.

The next book to be released involves Kurt Vonnegut, for instance. But the magazine can also take specific topics or historical events and create interesting new eBooks.

"We're not simply going to reprint material developed by some of our great writers but there will also be two other things we're going to do: topics over time covered, or specific historical events," Stupar said.

As Bush Brothers go, Shrub—George the Younger—is not bad. He's less mean and less right wing than his brother Jeb and smarter than his brother Neil. Of course he's a know-nothing little pipsqueak compared with Ann Richards, but then, Richards is pretty special. – Shrubwacked (1994)

"We have 15 or 16 of what we call Theme Packs, our own PDFs we can turn into eBooks. Things like the Brown v. Board of Education decision. We had unbelievable coverage of that... the Scopes trial, the Scottsboro case, and so forth."

The Nation, being a text oriented magazine, means that the words are paramount. So *Molly Ivins: Letters to The Nation* comes as a PDF or EPUB.

But *The Nation* is moving more and more into native platforms. Its iPad edition, The Nation Magazine, for instance, is built using the Mag+ platform – though its older app from PixelMags is still in the App Store, as well, and has been renamed The Nation Magazine – PixelMags Replica, differentiating it from the newer app. Eventually this native tablet edition will makes its way to the Android platform.

The new eBook, like the Gore Vidal book before it, was edited by Richard Lingeman, who writes the introduction.

If there can be a criticism of the latest eBook release, it would be that it is fairly short at 70 pages (the Vidal eBook is three times as long). One wants more, but knowing that there will be no more columns from Molly Ivins is still too painful a thought to contemplate for many admirers.

On the other side of the political spectrum, even Texas Gov. Rick Perry, who Ivins called "Governor Goodhair" wrote at the time of her death – possibly with his teeth clenched:

"Molly Ivins' clever and colorful perspectives on people and politics gained her national acclaim and admiration that crossed party lines."

(Originally published on TalkingNewMedia.com on July 15, 2013)

Update:

Like many newspaper or magazine publishers who have begun to create and publish their own eBook lines, *The Nation* has previously used partnerships to produce print books for a number of its journalists.

The Nation still maintains a separate book website, Nation Books, which hosts its line of books produced with The Perseus Group.

These books can be found as digital editions in the Apple iBook Store and on Amazon.com, where Nation Books is listed as the publisher and The Perseus Group as seller. These titles can also be found within eBookNation.

Section Three: Focus Publishing

For most print magazine publishers, extending their magazine brand means creating new products such as newsletters, books or events.

But photography magazines are unique in that they often have far more content than they can use in any given print edition of the magazine.

For example, a feature on a photographer may only have room for one or two examples of the artist's work. In the digital publishing environment, though, space is unlimited. One way to take advantage of this online or on tablets is to have photo galleries instead of simply one photograph.

Another way is to launch completely new digital

publishing products. The publisher of *Focus Fine Art Photography Magazine* has made the decision to launch new digital-only magazine titles – some of which are original content, and some of which one might label as custom publishing ventures.

Focus Publishing launches new digital magazine, *Exposures*, continues search for the perfect publishing platform solution for its ambitious media plans

Focus Publishing, which publishes *Focus Fine Art Photography Magazine,* has launched a new digital-only magazine into the Apple Newsstand, Exposures. The app launch is the third magazine title the publisher has launched in app form, and the second natively designed tablet magazine.

Exposures uses the Adobe DPS to create its interactive digital magazine, a solution that the publisher is not 100 percent satisfied with, but which gives the magazine more of the kinds of interactivity, navigation and design that they desire.

David Spivak, the president and publisher, told me that the first native digital magazine was Focus Folios, which was initially part of the main print magazine, but it was split off after Issue #19 of the main print title. Inside the new digital magazine Spivak explains why this was done:

"The reason for this was that in digital format, we could

allow our reading audience to enjoy a full perspective of a photographer's work without the print costs and page count being a factor," Spivak wrote in his Publisher's Letter. "In other words, Prior to Issue #19, the most number of pages a photographer was ever allowed in our Focus Gallery section, was eight."

Focus Publishing's first app was created by MagazineCloner, but the results were not satisfactory. The publisher still publishes issues for the app to serve the readers that have signed up, but the app itself was pulled from the Newsstand.

In March of last year a new app was launched through PixelMags. Those apps are replica editions of the print magazine, of course, as is the Zinio edition that was launched at the end of 2010.

But the publisher is now fully onboard the interactive magazine bandwagon. "In the future, we will continue to add limited amounts of interactivity to each issue of Focus Magazine, Focus Folios and Exposures and study the response that the interactivity generates. If we like it, we will think about creating fully interactive editions that sell separately from static-PDF versions of each title," writes Spivak.

"How can you scroll through interactive articles and slideshows while flipping through pages of dried ink? You can't. This is the benefit of having a digital magazine, and I think, after time many of you will adapt and enjoy the interactivity as much as I do."

As you will see in the video, Exposures is a fully interactive magazine, with animation, slideshows and video fully utilized in the digital edition. While Focus Folios covers subjects such as architecture, landscape and other art photography areas, Exposures is about the human form.

But inside this first issue you will immediately also notice the other photography magazine apps advertised. One of those is Pikturesque, which can be found in the Newsstand under the Focus Publishing name. This is part of the new direction the publisher is taking.

"We're launching a new service, working with a third party app development software, and this new service is going to allow us to create fine art photography magazines for other photographers," Spivak told me this afternoon. At least four are in the works.

"The photographer gets to showcase their work in a way that also allows them to earn a different source of revenue, a different source of income. To do this before digital media was completely impossible."

In addition to these projects, the publisher is also building digital publications for fine art galleries. One of these is already to be found in the App Store, the stand-alone app Joy Wai Gallery.

The plan is that, for a fixed price, galleries or photographers can have print-on-demand publications, a static PDF replica and/or an interactive edition. For now, this work is being done using Adobe's solutions, but the publisher told me that they are searching for something better, something that can do all that they would like.

"There is the old saying if you want it done right, do it yourself," Spivak said. So they are working with developers to come up with their own publishing platform – going a similar route, I suppose, as TRVL has with the launch of its PRSS publishing platform (see interview with the TRVL team here).

Exposures is a free download that will then give you access to the first issue found inside. The premiere issue is priced at $4.99, and subscriptions are available for $2.99 per two-month increments, or a semi-annual subscription for $10.99, and an annual subscription for $19.99 (not sure those prices really make sense).

(Originally published on TalkingNewMedia.com on March 4, 2013)

Update:

Since the publication of the piece on TalkingNewMedia.com, Focus Publishing has followed through on its promise to publishing additional digital editions and has released several new digital-only magazines.

The two most recent are Lenscape Magazine which features landscape photography, and Shifra Magazine featuring the photography of Shifra Levyathan.

Released earlier was Poses, a digital magazine that "brings the artist's model to your tablet," the app description says. "Each issue presents two models in a panoramic 360 degree pose, plus all the still images tablet from those panoramic poses, and a model's portfolio.

Focus Publishing has eight tablet applications inside

the Apple App Store as of March of 2014. Whether they have been able to attract readers is hard to tell as there are few reader reviews on these apps – something that is not that unusual, however.

DOUGLAS B. HEBBARD

Chapter Three:
Building A Digital Business

TRVL on the iPad

Section One: TRVL and PRSS

One of the most popular digital magazines so far released for the iPad, TRVL has been downloaded over a million times, according to its publishing founders, Jochem Wijnands and Michel Elings.

The original digital magazine app was launched in September of 2010, then updated in November of 2011 to move the app into the Apple Newsstand. But the biggest update occurred one year later when the publishing team decided to migrate the app off its original publishing platform onto a new platform that they had themselves developed.

Now the publishing team is offering that platform, PRSS, for use by other publishers.

Team behind the iPad magazine TRVL gets things ready for roll out of PRSS, its own tablet publishing platform

The travel iPad magazine, TRVL, first launched in September of 2010, has seen a number of updates of late – the reason for the updates is that the publishing team has recently moved the digital magazine off the Woodwing/Adobe platform it has used, onto a platform it has developed itself.

The transition has not been an easy one: TRVL is a unique app where a subscription to the magazine gives the reader access to over 80 editions (and counting). A subscription is not so much a way to access monthly magazines as it is a way to access the TRVL ecosystem.

TRVL

Launched by Dutch co-founders Jochem Wijnands, a documentary photographer, and Michel Elings, who is responsible for the design and technical portions of the digital magazine, TRVL has become instantly popular inside the Apple App Store, and later the Newsstand. The app has come to symbolize for many the potential of the tablet publishing platform.

TRVL emphasizes the photographer, not necessarily the travel writer, leaving the photography to speak for itself.

"We try to make the content feel really personal," Michel Elings told Susan Currie Sivek of MediaShift1 this summer.

"We don't crop photos, and we don't put text on photos. We respect the photographer and writer. We want to give people the feeling that a writer and photographer went to Amsterdam, and this is what they've seen."

"What is motivating us is the fact that these are historic times, and we can make a difference," Jochem Wijnands told TNM recently.

For the TRVL team, the launch of the iPad in 2010 opened up some unique opportunities.

"Our first reaction was 'wow, we can start our own magazine' – which used to be so difficult, and now it's easy," Wijnands said. "It was still quite a lot of money involved, but nothing compared to what you would normally need, and you could reach a readership all over the world."

TRVL's approach has been different from the start. Rather than creating a magazine based on print, where the design owes its inspiration from print travel magazines such as National Geographic or a Condé Nast title, and where each issue tries to give readers a broad range of topics, each weekly issue of TRVL concentrates on one destination, as seen through the eyes of the photographers whose work is featured in the issue.

"It's new magazines like ours that show that it is going to be a whole new game," Wijnands said of TRVL.

Publishing weekly also has tremendous advantages based on the way Apple's App Store works, the TRVL team believes.

"I don't think a monthly magazine works because you never use the algorithms of the App Store. When you publish new content, the App Store ranks you higher the next day, so when you publish, you are in a good position for the weekend. When you only do this once a month, you never use your advantage," Elings told MediaShift.

TRVL's first iPad magazine app was created using Woodwing's platform – a decision that must have seemed like a natural choice – WoodWing is based in Zaandam, just outside Amsterdam. But since TRVL first launched, WoodWing has changed its mission, now becoming a reseller

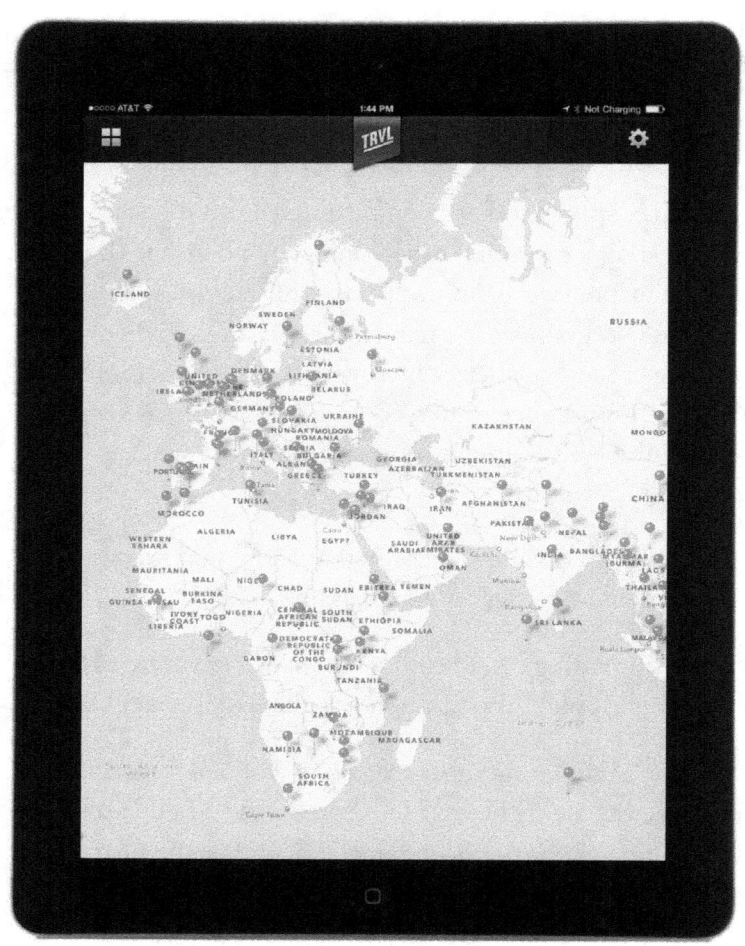

TRVL's map feature

of the Adobe platform and concentrating on enterprise solutions. The platform probably was never a good fit, in any case.

"We are really into less is more," Elings said. "I turned off 90 percent of what you can do with WoodWing because I don't think it helps the user."

So after almost two years of publishing, and over 700,000 app downloads, TRVL's co-founders felt they needed something else.

"So then we started developing our own software out of frustration with what was available," Wijnands said.

"If there was an acceptable software around about a year ago we would have seriously considered it."

PRSS

Later, the publishers of TRVL let word out that they would be entering the digital publishing platform business, offering its own publishing solution called PRSS.

Things have proceeded slowly, as the TRVL team works out the kinks within their own iPad magazine app.

Changing platforms for a tablet magazine is not exactly an easy thing to do – especially if you want to continue to offer the magazine's past issues to your loyal readers.

Some major publishers have resorted to launching separate apps for their archives when moving over to a new system. Hearst, for instance, has launched a stand-alone app (meaning not placed in the Apple Newsstand) to house the Esquire digital magazines of its tablet editions published from October 2010 to October 2012.

Meanwhile, its newly updated Newsstand app will house the brand new issues.

For TRVL, though, where all the issues are housed in one app and are part of the basic design of the app, it was necessary to redo all the issues using the new platform.

After they had recreated all the past issues using the PRSS platform, a major update to TRVL was issued.

"We could only test our app the minute we had actually gone live," Elings said.

"We designed 80 magazines in the four days before we went live."

"It was the first time we could see whether it was working the way we wanted it to. Then we saw some glitches, so we did another update almost immediately," Wijnands said. "Now we're preparing another update which should solve, say, 95% of what we're not happy with."

As the team fine-tunes its own app for TRVL it must now deal with the flood of inquiries it received once it announced publicly that it would offer PRSS to outside publishers. Soon the TRVL team will be making the rounds showing off PRSS and getting feedback from those firms and individuals interested.

"It's a philosophy that we are applying to iPad publishing," Wijnands said of PRSS.

"We've been thinking about this for two years and we've got the experience in publishing ourselves, so we know what we're talking about."

I asked Wijnands and Elings if the new platform is flexible enough to handle different kinds of publications, or would it be a one-trick pony, giving the publisher only a clone of TRVL?

"It's built to be flexible, it's built for the future, and it's built for the iPad – It's built for Apple," Wijnands assured me.

"And if you want to even take it a step further, I'd say it is built for the best user experience on whatever tablet or device you're going to publish."

"So the whole idea behind it is to create something that is perfect for the device you are publishing on."

For now the thought is that the team will launch PRSS in beta as a simplified version.

"What we mean by that is that all the stuff that can be done in TRVL can be done in that version," Elings explained.

Then, after getting more input, and more requirements, the team will add features.

For now, the thing to know about PRSS is that it is native to iOS. As a result, file sizes are smaller, and the things you would expect from any tablet edition – retina display support, interactivity, pinch-to-zoom, social sharing, analytics – are all present.

Coming soon will be translation services, regional targeting, e-commerce and other features.

The next thing to watch out for will be the next TRVL app update, which will fine-tune the app and signal that they are nearing the point when they can unveil PRSS to the public.

(Originally published on TalkingNewMedia.com on December 11, 2012)

Update:

After TRVL issued its update following this article's publication, the publishing team appeared to work out any bugs that might have remained in the app.

The Newsstand app now has well over 100 separate editions available within its library as of the late summer of 2013, and the app continues to get overwhelmingly positive reviews from readers.

As for PRSS, the platform was in beta with a select group of publishers through the summer and finally, on October 2, the platform was unveiled to the public at The Next Web Conference in NYC.

The first digital magazine, other than TRVL, that is using the platform is, in fact, The Next Web, which launched a brand new tablet magazine SHIFT by TNW.

SHIFT by TNW

The premiere issue of *Citygram* on the iPad

Section Two: Citygram

The common wisdom maintains that a tablet-only magazine start-up would have to target and appeal to a national or even international audience to succeed.

The reason behind this thinking is that no city or regional tablet magazine launch would be able to reach enough readers who own an iPad (or other tablet device) in order to profitably publish.

But the equation changes, possibly, when one talks about a community where high tech is king. There, one might hope, a tablet magazine start-up would be able to reach enough tablet owners - cities like San Francisco or Palo Alto... or Austin, Texas.

New publisher changes careers and launches a city magazine for Austin, Texas – Citygram

If traditional print publishers had illusions that the new digital platforms would only mirror those in the print world they only need to pay attention to the new apps launched each day into the Apple Newsstand to know that the competitive landscape is changing fast.

Not only are dozens of new digital-only publications

launching each week, but many are entering categories previously thought to only be of interest to local media companies – such as city/regional magazines.

Launched last week, Citygram is a new city magazine from Austin, Texas, published by Chris Perez under the developer name of Left Right Media LLC. The new digital magazine is a thoroughly professional looking publication that would easily be mistaken for a commercial release from a big name publisher – were it not for the fact that most city/regional magazines being released by the big publishers are actually dull, replica editions with little to offer new, younger readers.

For Chris Perez, the effort to launch Citygram meant a major career change, from engineer at IBM to new publisher.

"It's been a six or seven month operation from getting the concept to building the team to getting it live in the App Store," Perez told me on Friday.

"It required a lot of passion on my part. I was very interested in art, very interested in design and photography. And what appealed to me the most about the magazine format was it was connecting everything I knew."

While Perez may have grown up wanting to be an artist, a talk with his parents led him down a more practical path, studying engineering at Austin College, later getting a masters in engineering from the University of Michigan before joining IBM.

But Perez was determined to launch his own digital magazine and so went about deciding on the right digital publishing platform and sought funding. First he looked at the magazine he was reading digitally and wanted the same level of interactivity he found in his favorite titles.

"Why is there not interactivity across the board in magazine apps I read now – one's like Vanity Fair, GQ and Martha Stewart Living?" he asked himself. What he found out was that these titles were using the Adobe DPS to create their tablet editions (though he did look at some other options, as well).

"They had the experience I wanted," Perez said. "I definitely wanted to escape this vision of a digital magazine being a PDF export of print, and being a little hokey with animations and graphics. So I wanted to be professional – my bar (to reach) was to be those national publications on the look and feel. I wanted to be unchained from print, I want to be all digital."

Next Perez tried a Kickstarter project in hopes of raising $10,000. That effort did not succeed and so Perez had to fund Citygram himself.

"It is a little bit expensive. You have to come up with $6,000 up front to be in that professional realm," he said, referring to the cost of Adobe's DPS Newsstand solution. "And when people download it there is an expense, so that's tricky – that's going to be tough to juggle."

Complicating matters is the business model chosen to launch Citygram. The new digital magazine will be free of charge to download and will eventually be supported, Perez hopes, by paid advertising.

"You have to take the risk first, no one's going to put

money in your favor until you can show them you can release the product and have it out there."

(Originally published on TalkingNewMedia.com on May 13, 2013)

Update:

As if the challenges of succeeding with a city/regional tablet-only magazine were not difficult enough, with its second issue Citygram has gone weekly through the App Store update process. In this way the second issue now has several "sections" – separate downloadable sections published under the umbrella of Issue 2.

TALKING DIGITAL

Liz Castro – Photo: Lluís Brunet

Section Three: Liz Castro & ePub

The great thing about publishing one's own personal news website is that the publisher gets to decide what is news, what new apps to write about, and who to interview.

The publication of a book on the situation in Catalonia by Liz Castro was the perfect time to conduct an interview.

I had discovered Liz Castro through web searches for solutions to eBook publishing problems. Her website, Pigs, Gourds, and Wikis, is where Castro discusses issues with EPUB3, self-publishing, and other topics related to digital book publishing.

Castro is an expert at, and an advocate of EPUB 3, the current revision of the EPUB standard, which promises to bring more interactivity and layout flexibility to eBooks. EPUB is an open standard, and therefore stands in contrast to proprietary systems such as the Adobe Digital Publishing Suite or Apple's iBooks Author.

Castro asked me if I might write something about the book for TalkingNewMedia.com and I immediately agreed if Castro would allow me to interview her.

The interview was a great excuse to talk to Castro about a wide range of subjects very much of interest to me, including self-publishing, publishing standards, and print-on-demand.

An interview with Liz Castro, editor and publisher of *What's up with Catalonia?*

Author, editor, publisher and EPUB expert Liz Castro has recently published an important new book on Catalonia and its move towards independence from Spain, What's up with Catalonia?: The causes which impel them to the separation.

The book, available both in print and digitally, is a well-edited, highly informative, and easy and pleasurable to read collection of 35 articles concerning its subject.

The book's editor and publisher, Liz Castro, is perfectly positioned to organize, edit and produce this collection based on her technology publishing background, her translation skills, her time spent in Catalonia, and her digital publishing expertise.

Castro has gathered together an amazing group of experts, from politicians to authors, from academics to technology experts, to examine the history, culture and politics of Catalonia – and, most importantly, to examine the issue of separation from Spain.

A little background: last September 11, Catalonia's National Day, 1.5 million gathered in Barcelona in a pro-independence demonstration. What followed this event was snap elections where the issue of Catalonian independence became the central issue. The momentum that seemed apparent was the inspiration that led Castro to begin to organize this new book.

The articles were written in December 2011 and January 2012, and the book was quickly completed – just before the

Catalan parliament voted in favor of a Declaration of Sovereignty, according to Castro's editor's note to the book.

"Some of the writers who contributed articles for this book I knew previously, but others put their trust in me sight unseen," Castro writes. "I am indebted to both groups for their confidence, their collaboration, and their insights. I hope I have captured the spirit of their articles with my translations."

Castro's contributors include: Artur Mas, the president of Catalonia, who contributed the prologue to the book; Andreu Domingo, Deputy Director for Demographic Studies at the Autonomous University of Barcelona who contributes a fascinating report on immigration; and New Yorker J.C. Major who writes "On the prickly matter of language."

"What, then, makes a nation? Not race or religion—at least not for Catalans," writes Major. "Nor the trappings of power—a state, an army—whose unquestioned benefits they lost a long time ago. The right place to look for proof of Catalonia's unique personality is in the broad field of culture—in the set of values and customs that are shared by a community and are specific to it, the common way of doing things that is recognized as such by the people living in a certain land and also by those coming into contact with it for the first time."

Though the book takes a decidedly pro-independence point of view, the book is by the far the most up-to-date and thorough look at the issues involving Catalan independence, and is also a great example of how to organize and self-publish a book in both print and digital formats. The book is available on Amazon.com at $10.80 in paperback form and for $3.99 for the Kindle. It is also available inside the Apple iBook Store at the same price of $3.99, as well as at Barnes & Noble in both print and digital forms.

"I tried to make it so they could open the book any place and find an article that didn't put them off, was so hard to read and complicated and based on previous information, so they could jump right in."

Castro points to the anecdotal articles such as that by Josep Maria Ganyet and the article by Eva Piquer as contributions that are particularly good at covering topics for the lay reader.

I can't help but think that if Castro had spent her time in Athens rather than Barcelona we would be on the receiving end of a brilliant examination of the issues surrounding the crisis there. But we will gladly settle for this, and I highly recommend its purchase.

Ninety percent of the material in the book is new, Castro told me earlier this week while driving down to the IDPF conference in New York where she gave a presentation on EPUB3.

Following the September 11, 2012 demonstrations, Castro watched from the United States as events began to unfold. The president of Catalonia had previously campaigned on a platform of negotiating a new fiscal pact with Spain. But when this fell apart the issue of sovereignty began to become top of mind.

"Being from the United States, I was watching all of this

and noticing how it was getting huge amounts of press – and it was really exciting for me because I've been following Catalonia ever since I went to live there in the eighties and no one had ever talked about Catalonia in a political way... newspapers had never talked about Catalonia as a political entity, or very little, they mostly talked about football, they talked about food, and they talked about tourism and (Antoni) Gaudi," Castro told me.

Suddenly Catalonia was all over the press, and Castro thought that, at first, the media was doing a good job of covering the story.

"But as things got more complicated, and it wasn't just 'we're going to have another demonstration, tomorrow we're going to have a referendum then we're independent' the newspapers started to publish less, and the things that they published were not substantial enough," Castro said. "They mostly continued on the same theme of *Catalonia's rich and selfish, and not only that they're indebted.*"

So Castro started to think about publishing a book on the subject.

"This is something I can do," Castro concluded. "I can get up-to-date information about what's going on right now, not this old stuff, and I can make it a lot more nuanced, a lot more detailed, so people can really understand what's going on there."

"There's the question of language, of its history, the feeling of not belonging to Spain, not being appreciated, not being understood."

So Castro started her outreach to possible contributors.

"In the letter I said 'I'm not anybody, I'm a lay person in terms of Catalan politics, but I know how to make books. If you guys can write it, if you can get me good information, I can translate it, I can make it into a book. I can make it exist.' So that is what we did," Castro told me.

"These were amazing people, these were politicians, the opposition leader of the Catalan left, eventually the president of Catalonia decided he would contribute, there's top tier journalists, academics, sociologists. It is really quite an amazing collection of people. They're not famous in the United States, but in Catalonia everyone knows who every single one of the contributors is."

Liz Castro was able to tell readers of her blog that *What's up with Catalonia?* was available to download in early March. Castro was able to use her blog to explain where to find the book inside major online retail outlets, as well as that they could download the book directly from her.

Because the print form of the book is completely print-on-demand using Amazon's CreateSpace, as well as Lightning Source (Castro promises a blog post on using these two companies and I said I would love to re-post that blog entry here – I'm not sure she was enthusiastic about that), there was no need to fund a print run.

Instead, Castro used crowdfunding as a way of spreading word of the book and getting the end product into the right hands. Recently she guest contributed a nice post on the subject of crowdfunding on the Publishing Perspectives website.

"But my book posed a unique problem in terms of crowdfunding: the people who might be willing to sponsor the book — Catalans who wanted their story told — were not the target audience for the book. Americans, Brits, and other people outside of Catalonia with only a cursory idea of what was going on there, 13 million of whom visit Catalonia every year were the target," Castro wrote.

So, rather than using Kickstarter, Castro signed up at the Catalan crowdfunding site called Verkami. "My goal," Castro wrote, "was to raise enough money to send 500 copies of the book to libraries, magazines, and political leaders all over the world. And thus, the rewards consisted of the typical copy of the book for the sponsor, but much more importantly, one or more books sent to the recipients of the sponsor's choice.

Nearly 600 people sponsored the book, raising about $15,000.

For Castro, getting the book into the hands (or tablet) of the right audience is the goal. She is especially keen to get it into libraries but is finding it challenging, as libraries will not accept unsolicited books.

So far 20 to 30 bookstores in Barcelona are carrying the book – supplied by the UK division of Lightning Source – and Castro says she is pretty happy with sales so far.

Liz Castro found herself in a uniquely qualified position to publish *What's Up with Catalonia?* based on her background in technology publishing and her time spent in Barcelona.

"One of the first jobs I ever got about publishing was actually in Barcelona in a computer company that wanted to distribute Macintosh software, and so I started working in the publications department," Castro told me.

"One of our first projects was translating PageMaker 2.0 into Spanish and doing all the documentation. It's sort of a reflection of my whole life since then because I've been constantly working on documentation using the tools that I talk about. So here I was working on Spanish PageMaker but using PageMaker to do it with."

In the early '90s she started her own book publishing company providing translations of Mac software books in a market, Spain, with only about 50K Macs in it. It was with this experience that Castro learned the print business, dealing with print runs, distribution and the like.

Then she moved back to the U.S. in 1993 to work with Peachpit Press (sold in 1994 to Pearson PLC) on The Macintosh Bible (in English).

Following that project, Castro was asked to write a book on HTML, though she admits she knew little about HTML at the time – though she found the subject fascinating.

"It was an amazing thing because it was this way of helping regular people to publish their ideas and get their ideas out on the web to the public without a huge amount of infrastructure – and that's kind of been the theme of my employment over the years."

Then in 2010 came her book *EPUB Straight to the Point*.

"The web has been hard to commercialize for regular people. But books you can actually sell," Castro said. "The abilities that EPUB bring are that you don't need a huge infrastructure to make a book."

Also in 2010, Castro moved back to Barcelona and has since been able to combine her skills in eBook publishing to produce new books. One of those is Barcelona, *Catalonia: A View from the Inside* by Matthew Tree. The book is derived from the essays Tree had put on his website, and made into both a Kindle Edition and print book through Amazon.

"While this was going on, EPUB was evolving, and my feelings about publishing were evolving," Castro said.

"I was doing books for other people and still working with Peachpit to do my books. And one of the things that was hard for me – I don't mean to complain – but I was tired of doing HTML, I've been working on it since 1988," Castro told me. "It's gone through seven editions, it's gotten to be really big, it's gone from 140 pages to over 500 now."

"I've been really struggling with how to keep a book current without me redoing it. So when fixed layouts started to be a big thing – I think that was in December of 2010, only six months after the iPad was released, and only six months after *EPUB Straight to the Point* came out in June – Peachpit started talking about doing a second edition and I said 'wait a minute, I don't want to get into this cycle again.'"

"What if I just create a short, extra chapter about fixed layout itself? I was thinking about this for myself I can use this for promotional material for my book and I can use it as a way to keep the book current."

This new eBook can be bought separately, but is really meant to drive sales of the main title, as well as to keep *EPUB Straight to the Point* current.

This experience with EPUB, and her advocacy of the standard – which she advocates – has made her a valuable resource on the subject, as evidenced by her presence at the IDPF conference in New York (you can read a recap of her speech there this week on the Digital Book World website.

Update:

Liz Castro and her husband moved back to Barcelona in September of 2013 (she has been back and forth over 25 years, she told me).

On September 11, the region's national day, a mass demonstration occurred, organized by the Assemblea Nacional Catalana (Catalan National Assembly). On that day Catalans linked hands literally across the region – from El Pertús in the north, near the French border, to Alacanar on the Mediterranean Sea near Valencia.

Castro said she is now working on a Spanish edition for *What's up with Catalonia?*

"The people who really need information, like what was included in my book, don't read Catalan," Castro said. "That's why I wanted to make the book available in English, and why the next version I want to do in Spanish."

Castro said she also has plans for two other Catalonia-related book projects, as well as the completion of the delayed EPUB and Javascript books.

Liz Castro – Photo: Lluís Brunet

TALKING DIGITAL

Joe Zeff – Photo: courtesy Joe Zeff Design

Section Four: Joe Zeff Design

The first time I heard of Joe Zeff Design was when the magnificent app 'Above & Beyond: George Steinmetz' was released in early 2011.

The book app seemed to capture what was possible with tablet publishing better than most of the other efforts I had seen up to that point.

"This application teaches us that, even if you're using the same publishing tools as so many publishers out there, you can still make a difference by thinking out of the box and pay real attention to what the content needs," Talking New Media contributor Pedro Monteiro wrote at the time.

At the time Joe Zeff Design (JZD) was using the WoodWing Digital Magazine solution to build their apps. This soon changed when WoodWing became a partner with Adobe, forcing many of their customers to convert to the Adobe Digital Publishing Suite.

But the change has been a good one for JZD, and today JZD is listed on the Adobe website as a DPS Channel Reseller Partner.

An Interview with Joe Zeff

Like myself, Joe Zeff comes from the newspaper industry. Where as I moved from journalism to the business side of newspapering, Zeff went from the reporting side to design.

Zeff worked at the *Pittsburgh Post-Gazette* as a reporter before taking a position at the *Detroit Free Press* that allowed him to design news and feature pages. After two years Zeff moved on to *The New York Times* where he was a presentation editor. His first experience in the magazine business came in 1996 when he moved to *TIME* magazine where he directed information graphics at *TIME*, and introduced computer-generated illustration.

"When I was growing up I wanted to be the editor of a newspaper," Zeff told me in July of 2013. "I wanted to be the editor of my hometown newspaper, I wanted to do that since I was 11 years old. And I knew that to be the editor of the newspaper you needed to know every job, so I really approached newspapering from a very broad perspective. I tried to learn a little bit about everything. And along the way it turned out that, while I started out as a writer and an editor, it turned out that those skills really made me a fairly capable designer - whereas many designers came into the business, both in newspapers and magazines, with an interest in color and composition, my interest was in content. So I am able to design things that was perhaps more effective than some of my peers in telling a story."

"I worked at eight different newspapers in the course of eight years and during that time opportunities emerged to jump from the copy editing side and the reporting side of the business to the design side of the business. And once I was there, there was no turning back because I felt I could tell stories visually, with more impact, than I could as a writer. As a writer I could tell one story, as a designer I sort of had the ability to tell everybody's story, and I have the ability to organize them and emphasize certain elements in such a way as to deliver a very cohesive story to readers every day."

"And that's how it happened. I was working as a reporter, when another newspaper offered me an opportunity to be an editor who also had some layout responsibility – and quickly the needle shifted from being a reporter to being a designer, but I never stopped being a journalist."

"That's what I feel I still do on a daily basis, I still feel like, when I'm working on an app, and I'm doing reporting just like I did many years ago when I had a reporter's notebook in my back pocket and I was on the beat."

In 2000 Zeff created his own firm Joe Zeff Design, a design and illustration studio that originally concentrated on creating computer-generated illustrations for the covers of magazines such as *Newsweek*, *TIME*, *Esquire*, *Sports Illustrated*, and *Rolling Stone*.

For a brief period, from the fall of 2008 to the end of 2009, Joe Zeff served as Creative Director at Splashlight Studios.

"I think what is interesting is that in the first decade of this company we were perceived as being illustrators and animators, as well as story tellers. Our ability to create realistic 3D illustrations led to the opportunity to join forces with Splashlight.

"During the time when my company was nested within Splashlight we did an increasing amount of production, and it frustrated me. I felt that we no longer were telling the stories, we were telling other people's stories."

"Finally, that relationship came to an end and it just so happened to be when the iPad was coming to market, and it just seemed like a divine opportunity to pore everything I've been, and my team has been doing for the past 20 years into this new platform that takes the design, the illustration, the animation, the story telling, all the things we've been doing for so long, and bringing them all together on this amazing device. So the timing was ideal."

January 2010 not only was the end of Joe Zeff's involvement with Splashlight, but it was the month Apple unveiled the iPad to the world. In April the first iPads were delivered to buyers in the U.S., and by the end of May to European buyers.

"Around 2010, when I knew that our future was going to be in creating apps, I confronted a weakness that we had as a company, we had no programming capability."

"So at that point it was my thought that our future was going to rest in creating interactive advertising for publishers. At the time, *TIME* magazine was developing its iPad edition to come out in April 2010 when the device was first launched, and they were using a platform called WoodWing."

"I reached out to WoodWing and was able to immediately communicate to them my hope to be able to create apps…I mean when I looked at WoodWing I kind of fell in love. It's like 'wow, I can be a programmer." I was never able to build a website from scratch, I sort of missed that whole period, that whole opportunity."

"Then all of a sudden here comes the iPad and here is a way I can become a programmer. I was able to establish a partnership with WoodWing and using WoodWing we built the 'Above & Beyond' app, we built an app for Splashlight, we built some other applications."

"Then, all of a sudden, WoodWing and Adobe partnered, and our WoodWing experience was worthless because WoodWing was no longer a viable way for us to create applications – and DPS we had never touched. We had no idea what it could or couldn't do."

"We had seen from afar what *Reader's Digest* was doing, and what Wired had done. At first it was challenging, there were some new things to learn in terms of multi-state objects versus hotspots. There were functional differences between the platforms. There were a lot of things we had to learn very quickly. But once we learned it we were able to build very compelling apps that won Adobe's attention"

The apps created by Joe Zeff Design got everybody's attention. In addition to 'Above & Beyond: George Steinmetz', JZD worked with Touch Press on Solar System for iPad, released in December of 2010. Then 'March of the Dinosaurs' the next year. JZD worked with *Everyday Health* on a diabetes app, 'Type 2 Diabetes: What Now?'

But it was the app 'The Final Hours of Portal 2' that was prominently featured by Apple in its App Store and probably convinced Adobe that JZD was one of its best examples of a designer working with the Adobe DPS.

"We are listed on Adobe's website as a reseller of their product but we have not resold very many of their products, but it's a good relationship because we are able to answer a lot of the questions that people who are interested in Adobe DPS have to ask. And that relationship has strengthened over the past year or so as Adobe has ventured outside of traditional publishing and so have we."

"It's a very healthy partnership, but it is important to note that we don't use Adobe DPS because they put us in their marketing, and they don't pay us to do this."

"We use Adobe DPS because it is the best tool for the job, and if something else came along that was better I would consider that. At the end of the day, I want to be able to create the best product for our clients and that requires a certain of agility that Adobe DPS gives us."

In addition to apps that are essentially eBooks, JZD has worked with magazine publishers to create both mobile and tablet edition apps. JZD worked with Ziff-Davis on the *PC Magazine* for iPad app that resurrected the title after it had ended its print magazine. The design firm also helped create the 'National Geographic for iPhone' app.

It's biggest ongoing magazine project, though, is the 'Fast Company for iPad' app for Mansueto Partners, which JZD produced each month through the first 13 issues.

"Here you had a forward thinking technology magazine that didn't have any presence on the iPad. They approached us with interest in creating a digital publication.

"We had worked with *Fast Company* through the years on

the editorial side in creating cover artwork and illustrations for the magazine. We certainly had a relationship before we started working together on the iPad."

"We jumped at the opportunity because it was a chance to take a very popular magazine that wasn't bound by a larger publishing company."

"It was a great opportunity for us. We were able to get involved with them on every level: from helping to identify what's the best way to pursue artwork so it works really well in print as well as on the tablet; we were involved in their planning meetings… It wasn't just a case where they would design a magazine and hand it over and we would make an iPad version. We were involved with the thought process to the magazine from start to finish."

"The biggest thing that we learned over the past year and a quarter is that communication is so important. The idea that, having that initial conversation that launches editorial and photography and videography, in a group setting that includes those that are involved with the web and the app and the print magazine and the events and marketing people."

"We spent as much time with the marketing department and the publisher as we did with the editors and photographers and writers. That type of inclusiveness allowed us to pursue much grander projects"

"We were involved on one project where we were with Lincoln to produce some interactive advertising that also involved editorial folks. That was something that wouldn't have been possible on Day One. It is really a matter of establishing a plumbing within an organization so that all of the efforts are being exploited on every platform and every way to achieve the greatest impact," Zeff said.

It has been over three years now since the introduction of the iPad and both JZD and the nature of digital publishing has changed considerably over that time.

"I find that our trajectory changes from quarter to quarter here as the market evolves. When we did 'Above & Beyond: George Steinmetz' it was a different world. At that point we were stretching our legs and trying to identify the best ways to leverage a new platform, a new way to communicate. Since then we've learned a lot."

"Hopefully there is a timelessness in everything we do. The idea of engaging a user doesn't really change from one year to the next. Good content is good content. And if you are more focused on telling a story than leveraging the capabilities of a specific device in a specific time frame, then you're able to create products that have longevity."

"One thing that has changed quite a bit is that there were far fewer consumers of tablet content. But as the number of consumers has increased, their interest in paying for content seems to have decreased. So it's really started to shape the business models that surround our apps."

"I really blame magazine publishers for contributing to the idea that interactive content on the iPad is free. In other words, I think there was an opportunity for the magazine industry to set some boundaries regarding the cost of interactive content. Some publishers chose to give away their content to help support their print subscriptions, and in doing so it really made it very difficult to start charging for

National Geographic for iPhone

some content when such a vast array of high quality applications were available for free for what you are already paying for."

"I think that has really obscured the vision for publishers, it has created a target that isn't necessarily the best target long term for magazine publishers. Instead of building interactive products in such a way that they generate new revenue, there has been much more of a focus on creating interactive applications that support a failing product, which is a product in decline, the venerable print magazine."

"I understand that rate base has been the way that magazines can quantify their value to advertisers but that is changing fast and to be fixed on that as your metric versus so many opportunities to create so many new products for so many new consumers and capture so much new ad revenue seems to be really short sighted. "

"I think some magazine publishers have been more proactive than others in seizing opportunities to innovate while others, to my astonishment, are still looking in the rearview mirror and trying to figure out how to support the brands that have covered their paychecks for the last 30 years. That is not the same way these magazine companies are going to generate revenue in the next 30 years, or even the next three years," Zeff said.

But Joe Zeff's opinions of what is possible from a commercial prospective inside the Apple App Store and Newsstand may be changing. What looked like a great business opportunity to land sales may be evolving to one

Photo: courtesy Joe Zeff Design

where the motivation for creating a new app may be more about marketing and brand extensions than simple sales.

"In 2010 I believed you could create a digital product and make money by selling it. I've learned three years later that that's not the best way to monetize an app. "

"I've learned that there are many business models that can be applied to application development that are much more effective than deriving revenue from one consumer sale after another. That might include sponsorships, that might include using apps to promote other revenue generators, that might include developing apps that build a brand. But that is one big takeaway - that selling apps to consumers is a very challenging task. Selling applications to marketers makes a lot more sense. Marketers are already allocating funds to deliver a message. "

"Tablets, and applications that are built to leverage the capabilities of those tablets, to a fast growing audience, are an incredibly effective way for marketers to deliver those messages."

Joe Zeff Design has evolved to a point where it is a training ground for new talent who move on to become art directors and app developers for magazine and newspaper companies.

"This is boot camp. We're working on three or four different projects that are starting from a blank sheet of paper."

"People who have worked here tend to go out into new environments and find that they are extremely well prepared.

Because here everybody who works here is involved in the entire lifecycle of a project: from here is someone we might pitch an app to; here is what we have discovered; here are some opportunities; here is how we should design it; here is how we should produce it; let's jointly decide the best way to market it; let's do the metrics together to see what is working and what isn't. "

"When you go into a magazine you may have access to one sliver of that span, whereas here, there is not only a sense of how to build an app, but why to build an app. "

"What's been interesting to me has been with our recent hire of Neil Jamieson from Time Inc. is that now it is starting to go in the other direction, to where people are looking to us – 'wow, this is the place I want to work.' "

"As I talk to people who are still working within large media organizations in New York City, they look at us and feel some sense of envy that we get to do all the fun stuff. I don't know, to me getting three weeks paid vacation and a company health plan sounds like fun. But I do think that everyone who works here feels a sense of ownership of everything we do and that's something that simply doesn't happen in a large organization."

Zeff's own role at JZD has changed in the last three years as the company has grown, and multiple projects are worked on each day.

"One thing I didn't expect, one thing I've learned in the last three years is that marketing an app is as much work as building an app. You have this burden of selling the app (to the client), then producing the app, then letting people know you did the app. All three of those jobs are demanding. It's forced me to reinvent myself, and refocus my company. I've had to hire some people to take on some of the creative responsibilities that were the very reason for starting the company in the first place. I don't think I fully realized three years ago how each of those three parts of my job were going to grow into three full-time jobs."

"In some ways our company has grown by making what appears to be sound decisions along the way, but in some ways we've just been caught up in the surf. Digital publishing just continues to become a bigger and bigger business and we're moving in the right direction. For the first ten years we were making illustrations for print magazines and going against the surf, and now we're rolling with the tide."

Chapter Four: The Rest

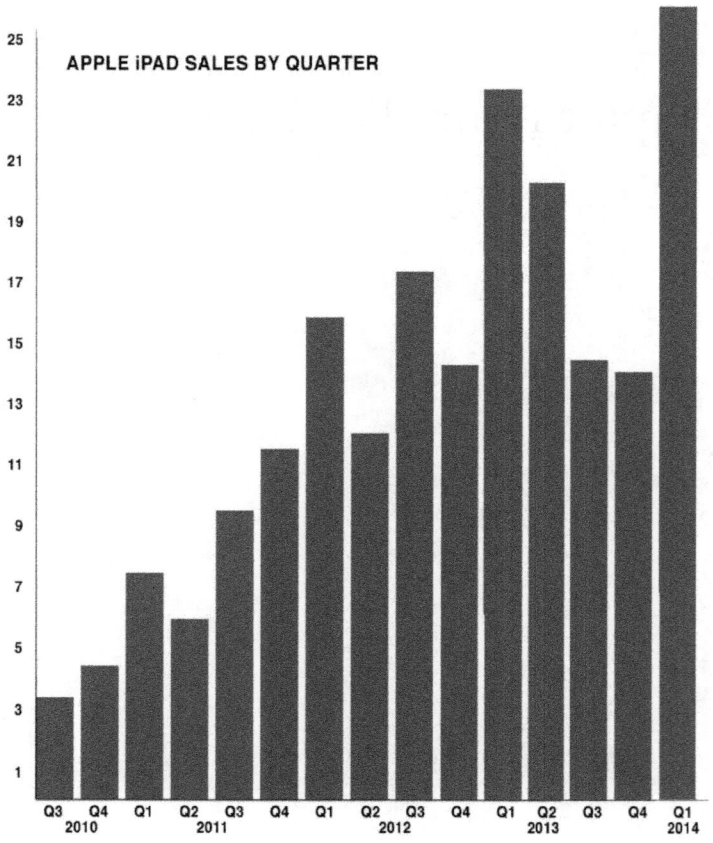

Section One: Known Unknowns

There are known knowns. These are things we know that we know. There are known unknowns. That is to say, there are things that we know we don't know. But there are also unknown unknowns. There are things we don't know we don't know.
– spoken by a soon-to-be former Secretary of Defense

With thousands of mobile applications having been developed and released by newspaper, magazine and book publishers, and with the Apple Newsstand jammed with titles, one might think that publishers would feel that the new digital platforms are already mature. But that is certainly not the case.

Behind the outward expressions of enthusiasm lie some severe doubts, as even those who have enjoyed tremendous success with their apps are turning cautious in regards to the commercial potential of the existing digital newsstands.

What we know is that consumers have been buying smartphones and tablets in large numbers and they appear to enjoy using them. Since April of 2010 to the end of September 2013, Apple had sold over 169 million iPads worldwide. IDC is predicting that over 200 million tablets will be sold worldwide in 2013.

But how many of these are being used to read books, newspapers or magazines? How many readers prefer digital publications, and in what format?

A survey of readers several years ago, conducted by a digital newsstand and a research company, showed that readers were eager to experiment with the new digital devices, but it also showed that most still preferred the print platform over digital devices. But even in 2010, the research showed that when reading a book or magazine, the reader wanted the platform to allow for leisurely reading, that is why online reading of these kinds of publications placed last, with eReaders and tablets performing better than all other ways of reading... other than print.

That assumption, that tablets would be the most important device for future development, has guided both book and magazine publishers these last three years.

I recently engaged in a brief Twitter discussion with TalkingNewMedia.com readers following a post on the problem of "discoverability" of Newsstand apps. While most agreed that for them discoverability was their number one obstacle to success, a couple of readers begged to differ. For them, the issue that was paramount was the number of tablets in the market. Not surprisingly, this was because they were publishers outside of the U.S., Western Europe or Australia. This is a good reminder that we are still very much in the middle of things. Publishers in the U.S. no longer think the market is too small to produce a tablet edition, though they may still wonder if they can reach their target audience efficiently through a Newsstand or Google Play app (this is especially true with B2B publishers).

At the risk of offending those that hate sports analogies, I think that it would be accurate to say we are still in the tablet and mobile publishing platform's preseason. Publishers are still experimenting and learning the platforms. The only real losers in any preseason are those who do not play.

The real risk for any publisher today is sitting still. Those that thought themselves wise to sit on the sidelines waiting for the tablet publishing platform to mature, for instance, can now feel sure that they are three years behind those companies which have been launching digital magazines and eBooks. Yes, maybe they can try to absorb the lessons that are being learned by other, more adventurous publishers, but they have not built the skill sets in their organizations that will be necessary to succeed in the future.

Many publishers have opted to outsource their mobile and tablet publishing products – including a number of companies that proclaim themselves digital first. As a result, they have been able to brag that they have launched new apps, but what have they really learned about app development, digital publishing platforms, app analytics, and the like?

One thing all the company executives whose interviews are featured here have in common is that they all risked it, they all tried (and are trying) to figure it all out.

My guess is that three years from now those companies that are featured here in Talking Digital will still be around, experimenting, serving their clients, their readers.

When I first started in the newspaper business a veteran of many years told me that it takes at least three years to start to finally *get it*. I'm not sure what he meant by *get it*, but I certainly know that after three years of working at the *Los Angeles Herald Examiner* I felt that I understood the business better and felt like a true newspaper professional.

It's been almost four years since the original iPad was launched, over six years since the introduction of the original iPhone. Those pursuing the new digital publishing platforms may not yet *get it*, but they are getting there.

TALKING DIGITAL

Section Two: About the Author

Douglas B. Hebbard is the publisher of the digital publishing news and information website TalkingNewMedia.com.

Launched in 2010, TNM has been covering mobile and tablet publishing since the launch of the original iPad, concentrating on news involving the newspaper, magazine and book publishing industries, and specializing in information on new tablet publishing efforts.

Hebbard is originally from Harper Woods, Michigan. He received his journalism degree from Central Michigan University and immediately headed to the west coast where he first worked for Hearst Newspapers at the Los Angeles Herald Examiner. Later he worked at Copley Los Angeles Newspapers at the Santa Monica Outlook.

Hebbard moved to Northern California in 1988 to work for what was then Lesher Communications at the Valley Times in Pleasanton. In late 1991 he was recruited to the McGraw-Hill Companies in San Francisco where he published a daily newspaper for the construction trades. There he launched a monthly magazine and never returned to newspapering, eventually moving to the Chicagoland area to publish trade magazines at Scranton Gillette Communications and later Reed Business Information (then known as Cahners Business Information).

Hebbard formed TNM Digital Media LLC in mid-2013. The new digital publishing firm's mission is to publish interactive eBooks and digital magazines of both original content and custom publishing projects for other media firms and brands.

The first eBook published by TNM Digital Media was *A Darker Sun – photographs by Dean Brierly*. Brierly is the editor of Black & White, a fine art photography magazine published by Ross Periodicals.

Recently released was *One Person Rally: I Have Something to Say*, a photographic series by Petra Sith.

Also published was a single-issue tablet magazine app, designed for digital publishing professionals: *Tablet Publishing - Winter 2013*.

All three digital media products can be found inside the Apple iTunes store.

Hebbard is married to Esther, has two daughters, and lives in northern Illinois with an aging basset hound named Cody.

ACKNOWLEDGEMENTS

Talking Digital was conceived as one of three digital publishing experiments to be conducted in the summer and fall of 2013.

The first of these books, mentioned in the About the Author section, was *A Darker Sun*.

The book you hold in your hand was supposed to be published soon after, but work on the digital magazine app, *Tablet Publishing – Winter 2013*, proved far more challenging than original thought, and so *Talking Digital* was put on the back burner. It eventually appeared inside the Apple iBooks Store as an interactive eBook in January 2014.

I would like to thank Mag+ and Bonnier for the use of the photography that appears here, as well as other material that appears in the eBook. Kara Udziela was very helpful is securing the material.

Liz Castro connected me with Lluís Brunet who provided the photography included in the interview with her.

Joe Zeff has been very generous with his time and in providing me with artwork for both this book and other projects.

Finally, a thank you to my wife Esther who has been very patient and supportive these past four years while publishing TalkingNewMedia.com.

About TNM Digital Media LLC:

TNM Digital Media is a publishing start-up company. Publishing projects include books, eBooks, digital magazines, and the digital publishing website TalkingNewMedia.com.

You can find the online bookstore at the website URL www.tnmdigitalmedia.com.

www.ingramcontent.com/pod-product-compliance
Lightning Source LLC
Chambersburg PA
CBHW051715170526
45167CB00002B/669